The Cross of Karma

Comment on Papyrus Oxy V 840

Frank Ludwig

Imprint

BoD Books on Demand 2015
Publishing and Print: BoD – Books on Demand, Norderstedt.
First English Edition (September 2015)
Copyright © 2015 Frank Ludwig
Cover design Frank Ludwig
ISBN 9783738641240
All rights reserved. No reproduction without permission allowed.

Dedicated to Jesus of Nazareth and the evolution of believe.

"Look, I make all things new."

(Jesus of Nazareth)

"For whatsoever a man soweth, that shall he also reap."

(King James Bible, Epistle to the Galatians, 6:7, "the first law of Karma")

…for they love the tree (and) hate its fruit, and they love the fruit (and) hate the tree….

(Gospel of Thomas, Log. 43:3)

Content:

1. Papyrus Oxyrhynchus 840 — 7
2. Comment on the Papyrus — 9
3. How to become clean inside — 10
   - 3.1 The sacrament of baptism — 13
   - 3.2 The ritual of confession — 13
   - 3.3 Prayer — 14
   - 3.4 Atonement — 15
   - 3.5 H'Oponopono — 15
4. Stay clean — 16
   - 4.1 The Ten Commandments — 17
   - 4.2 Comment on The 10 Commandments — 18
   - 4.3 Personal ethic — 25
   - 4.4 Do not consume "wrongly" — 26
5. A cleaning-ritual — 27
6. The harvest: What it means to be clean — 30
7. The Cross of Karma — 31

1. Papyrus Oxyrhynchus 840

"A certain Pharisee, a high priest called Levi, came and met them and said to the saviour:
„Who has permitted you to trample this sanctuary and to view these holly vessels, when you have not washed nor indeed you have your disciplines bathed their feet? Although you are defiled you have trampled this temple, a place that is so clean, where no one else walks or dares to look to look upon these holy vessels without washing and changing his clothes."

Immediately the saviour stood with his disciplines and answered him:
„You therefore who are here in the temple, are you clean?"

That one said to him, „I am clean, for I washed in the pool of David, and by onset of steps I went down in the water and by another I came up; and I put on clothes that are withe and clean. Then I came and looked upon these holy vessels."

The saviour answered him and said:" Woe to you blind who do not see. You have washed in these waters that have been poured out, in which dogs and swine have wallowed night and day. And when you washed your scoured outer skin, which even prostitutes and flute girls anoint, wash, scour and beatify for human lust.

But inside they are full of scorpions and every evil. But my disciplines and I, whom you say have not bathed, have been dipped in waters of eternal life, which come from …But woe to those….""

(Papyrus Oxyrhynchus 840)

2. Comment on the Papyrus

What is the point Jesus want to make clear here?
I think it is obvious that he states that although outer tidiness might be of advantage, the inner tidiness is the most essential thing a follower of Jesus might achieve. Jesus was always a man of the "inner kingdom."
"Teshuvah" he said and that means
"turn inside" or "return to the inside ".
From this standpoint it is clear that Jesus sets the priority to the "**tidiness inside**". A short explanation might serve the understanding of the reader.

Man is bound to act while in the world. Some people have fast lives and therefore have to act a lot. "New York, Rio, Tokyo". Some people have slow lives, the sit and meditate all day long and do not need to act so much. They are like the turtle, which is said to live for long. But even then man has to act. **Acting brings Karma.** Karma is the probably quantum-mechanical answer to action. Like a particle and its anti-particle the energy of the action and the energy of the Karma disintegrate and jump into different directions. They divide and the same time they are still connected.

And even non-acting might be "punished" somehow, since if the learning situation for the soul is made to act in a certain way, it is essential for you to act.

You can burn karma by action. **When the fruit of the action ripens the action is closed out against the karmic reaction.** If you have sinned a lot, you have a lot of "bad" karma, which means that you have dark energy patterns inside of you. You store karma until it ripens and it then brings situations forward that make you learn not to sin.

But when the lesson is learned, karma is no longer necessary, but dysfunctional since it punishes a person although it learned to behave in a different manner. **To punish is not the intent of God.** The intent of God is evolution and realisation of the spiritual potential of a person.

What are ways to reduce "bad" karma? Are there any? There are of course ways, otherwise a sinner never could become a saint.

3. How to become clean inside

Humans are like swimmer or people who bath in a ripping river. The river is called Samsara.

The humans are entangled in creepers on the ground of the river. These creepers are the dangerous feelings of envy, jealousy, greed, hate and anger. The water bites in the eyes and lets the people not see the things and how they are clearly, so they think everything what they can do, the should do and that the goals justifies the means and such stupid things.

Additionally the bodies of humans are weighted with a heavy burden called karma, which comes from earlier actions that draws them further down.

It is a disgusting picture of billion drowning people fighting and struggling for survival in this river of samsara.

Only some Bodhisattvas have learned to swim, and by the strength of their mind to lift some others who where drawing. Some even fewer Buddha you can see walking on the water. They are the ones that reach the other shore by dry feet.

Jesus knew how to walk on water and he even was able to teach this to his disciplines. So there is good news. First it is possible do so and second you can learn it.

"Can you walk on water? "

3.1 The sacrament of baptism

First there is the ritual or **sacrament of baptism**. It is done similar to the way John did it with water. The mind or soul of the person should be washed to clean it from sin or karma. Nowadays this is merely an empty ceremony since no priest is educated to wash sin away and no priest is a master like John was who laid the glimpse of enlightenment into the soul of the baptised. With John, baptism was an initiation into the spiritual world since the master put divine energy into the crown chakra and it was like starting the process that leads to God by awakening the baptised on a soul level. Real baptism leads to a consciousness that is wake to the soul.

3.2 The ritual of confession

The Catholic Church uses the ritual of **confession**. The believer tells the priest what he think he did wrong, where he could not meet the standard the church sets to meet Jesus demands. This is a handing over of both sin and responsibility to the priest. It is used since it is clear that no one is born a saint and to become holy you need to progress on the path and to stay clean or become even cleaner than before.
So to reduce sin or karma (the concept of sin and that of karma are pretty much the same) in the life of a believer

is accepted and used by the Catholic Church.
There are other ways to reduce sin or karma.

"Jesus washing sins away"

3.2 Prayer

First there is **prayer** in which the believer asks for forgiveness. **"And forgive us our debts, as we forgive our debtors."** (Mathew 6:12)
Sin and forgiveness are therefore close related. You can ask for forgiveness but it doesn't mean necessarily that the other person forgives you. But you did your share

and a graceful God, if you believe in such, will take always your effort into account. It is a bit like in Goethe's quote "whoever endeavours consequently will be released."

3.3 Atonement

A more complete concept to handle karma is that of **atonement**. For atonement, you first have to ask for **forgiveness**, you **give a compensation** for the pain or damage suffered by the other person and you **promise to change the dysfunctional behaviour** for the better. That changes the situation, the karma is less or gone if you do it often enough and it is shown that you learned the lesson.

3.4 H'oponopono

A beautiful prayer for forgiveness is that of **H'oponopono**:

"Please forgive me,
I am sorry,
I love you,
I thank you,
I give it to God and expect a miracle,
And I promise to do better from now on."

It is from Hawaii and it is said to put things again in the

right place. If you integrate it into atonement, it is the best prayer I do know.

If you came more on a grounded level, everything that detoxes your energy-system will reduce your suffering. So does sports. Walking, swimming and so on releases big amounts of negative energies that sum up to karma. "In a healthy body there lives a healthy soul."

4. Stay clean

The second point Jesus wants to make clear is, that regular cleaning of the inside is important, but not to become dirty is important as well. If you have company with dogs and swine and behave like them, it is more probable to become dirty. The Buddha recommended keeping the right company if you are not very grounded on the way.

This does mean too not to wallow in feelings or greed, hate, anger, jealousy and envy. It is human that these feelings might rise once in a while, but it is the task of the aspirant to transcend the perception of situations in which these feelings rise. They are poisonous for the mind and the spiritual development and they destroy as dysfunctional elements every relationship. So to work on you, to change for the better and to ascend is the second aspect in being clean.

4.1 The Ten Commandments

The Ten Commandments that where given by Moses are a guiding hand:

1. I am the Lord thy God (Ex. 20:2)
2. Thou shalt have no other gods before me (Ex. 20:3)
3. Thou shalt not make unto thee any graven image (Ex. 20:4-6)
4. Thou shalt not take the name of the Lord thy God in vain (Ex. 20:7)
5. Remember the sabbath day, to keep it holy (Ex. 20:12)
6. Thou shalt not kill (Ex. 20:13)
7. Thou shalt not commit adultery (Ex. 20: 14)
8. Thou shalt not steal (Ex. 20; 15)
9. Thou shalt not bear false witness against thy neighbour (Ex. 20:16)
10. Thou shalt not covet your neighbor's house, wife or anything else (Ex. 20:17)

4.2 Comment on the Ten Commandments

1) I am the Lord thy God (Ex. 20:2):

God is the absolute, the final and the indescribable.

2) Thou shalt have no other gods before me (Ex. 20:3)

Above God the almighty, there are no other Gods. There might be gods and goddesses on a lower plain or level below. This is an integral aspect of monotheism: There are other Gods, but they are below the Almighty. They do serve the Absolute Divine in many ways and are like transformation stations that transform the indescribable high energy or vibration of God into lower vibration until even man can bear them. In my understanding God is like the cosmos (in German "All"). The German "All" means all or everything. There I nothing outside "all", which in turns includes everything. The cosmos might contain several universes which are synonym for lower gods. And these universes consist of even more galaxies, which contain a billion suns. In Indian, "Paramatman" is the "Over soul" which contains all souls. So the All contains every soul, even that big souls of big gods and goddesses. Jesus sais in the Gospel of Thomas about the universe: "It is like a mustard seed

3) **Thou shalt not make unto thee any graven image (Ex. 20:4-6)**

This is a very important point, since if you make an image of God, you have an expectation. Expectations are seldom fulfilled especially if you put pressure on it. Not to have an image of God, not to have an expectation of a situation means that you and your mind are "innocent like a child". You leave God the lead. This might seem difficult especially if there are others around who have different expectations of the outcome of a situation.
And you usually love to make plans and to set goals. But then when you are at the point of being a good planner and successful in reaching your goals, you are asked to let go of even this.

And not to make an image of God is wise. Look, you made yourself an image of God, which is understandable. It was first only an image, then it became an institution that you call "xyz Church".

I said "When you imagine an image of God, it is like you put it in front before God. You then see only the image, but no longer God ITSELF. Now many of you see only the church, and no longer the true proportions and characteristics of God.

Like the poster of a person that is bigger than the face

and that is standing before the face of God ad you see only the poster and not the face any longer. It fits even better in German language. You say "Stell dir kein Bild von Gott vor." (Do not make yourself an image that you put in front of God.") "Vorstellen" means both "to imagine" and "to put in front of."

4) Thou shalt not take the name of the Lord thy God in vain (Ex. 20:7)

That s clear, isn't it? Or not… It means that you do not misuse the name of the lord. But….in every interpretation of the divine, there is implicitly the name of God as quotation there. And even the holiest church cannot speak the truth of God, it can only interpreted what is known about God. Therefore "Popes to err." The Pope is a chosen human. Humans can err. So the Pope can err". There where times when this was not so clear. And you should not misuse the name of God in other ways of course.

5) Remember the Sabbath day, to keep it holy (Ex. 20:12)

If God needs a rest, how do even man need a rest after working. So there must be time for recreation.

And there needs to be a time to cherish the divine. If you cannot or do not cherish the divine, which is the true good, then you do not cherish anything of value.

Jesus broke the fifth commandment. He healed a man on a Sabbath. The high priests of course said "he is sinning".
But first there are priorities and second there is freedom. Priorities put life first, then law.
Freedom says that Jesus has the free will to chose his day to rest and cherish the divine. By the way he rested probably his whole life ("in God") and second he cherished God with every action he did. You can do that too: "devote every action to God". You can bring no shit to God, that is clear. So you will probably devote only the best to God. By doing so, you do not collect no negative karma neither. If you devote all your actions to God, a form of "Bakti-yoga", then you do not get binding karma.

6) **Thou shalt not kill (Ex. 20:13)**

This is clear too: You shall not take away life.
"In dubido pro vita." When in doubt, chose life.

This is clear in the case of humans. No doubt.
Don't make war - make love.

But it is written, "Thou shalt not kill." That means neither humans nor animals. To kill, even an animal is sin and brings karma. Think twice even before you become a butcher. It brings a lot of karma to kill animals. A soldier collects in the worst case of a war even much more karma. If you only sell meat, you collect some but less karma. If you only save life, you collect no karma.

Even eating meat brings karma, be it only less than if you kill the animal yourself.

Hunting is no sport; in fact it is a sin. "Thou shalt not kill." All life is holy and from God.

Man is not perfect and it is normal to collect some karma. So people eat meat and fish. Fish do feel the death too, they have fear and do panic when killed. I myself am trying to become vegetarian. Some people need meat for their body, at least once in a while. But I stopped to by meat from the mass production of animals. These farms are like KZ's for living beings that feel pain, suffering and fear there. And when you eat the meat, think twice: It is flesh from some body that wanted to live.

There is only one thing I know that lessens the karma from eating meat or fish: To bless the animal from which it is. Say " Might you have a better incarnation in your next life" to the animal that died for your lunch.

There are other sins or karma from killing:

If you kill yourself, you are sinning. It brings you a lot of karma and you sit with the same problem in the next life.

The oath of hippocras therefore is one of the most holly ones.

7) <u>Thou shalt not commit adultery (Ex. 20: 14)</u>

You shall not betray your woman or man. That is easy to understand and sometimes difficult to obey too when your feelings go into a different direction and you love a married person.

Jesus himself rescued Magdalene from being stoned. Why?
First there were only accuses that Magdalene had committed adultery. Accuses do not have to be the truth. Even a judge can fail and even thousand judges can fail, if you see the judgement of the people over Jesus and Barabbas. So no punishment without a fair trial in an independent court should be allowed

Second "not to kill" is higher a commandment according to Jesus than "not to commit adultery." "In dubido pro vita."

8) Thou shalt not steal (Ex. 20; 15)

That is a clear one too. You shall not take away the property of another man.

9) Thou shalt not covet your neighbor's house, wife or anything else (Ex. 20:17)

That's an interesting again. You shall not covet. That means you shall not want to have something that is not yours or "even worse" you shall not covet at all. If you covet, you are attached and attachment is one of the main reasons for sin and karma. To covet sows much karma, and little of it is good.

10) Thou shalt not bear false witness against thy neighbour (Ex. 20:16)

Clear to. You shall at least not knowingly talk wrongly about another person.

4.3 Personal ethic: Your personal immune system for not to sin

Everybody has a personal ethic, at least should have. If no personal ethic is guiding you, you can even apply moral, although moral is rigid and "moralin" is a strong poison. Moral is what other people say what is good, and therefore second best if you are a complete human who can decide for yourself. Moral is like a vaccination.

Once there was a even deeper rooted consciousness that shows in the noun "taboo". A taboo, is a very deep "don't", that doesn't need even to be explained or be written. Cannibalism is still one of the taboos, although in modern society the economy is build accordingly cannibalistic. But today, many people have lost the idea of what is holy.
The best example is sexuality. Sexuality between man and woman is holly if it is saint, means non-hurting in a manner of exchange of tenderness called "love-making".

But man became perverted. In a time where the natural sexuality between a man and a woman is condemned, it is the policy of the church to allow the sexual intercourse between two men. This seems to me a kind of perverted.

Sex is made the master-sin that is made guilty for all other sins. If you study the masterpiece of Michelangelo at the ceiling of the Sistine Chappelle, you see the two, Adam and Eve, seduced by the snake. Then not the one who was responsible for the mistake, namely the snake, was thrown out of the paradise but Adam and Eve.

You see, this is the pattern shown often when sin occurs. The wrong person is made guilty and the guilty is spoken innocent. See Jesus and Barabbas.
So it is with sexuality. Sex is the condemned, but in fact another behaviour is the sin.

Without wanting to condemn, we live in a society where you can sell a car or whatever with sex, but sexuality and tenderness between man and woman, especially if naked (like god made man and woman) is a sin. Sex is made a monster. But be calm, it is only seen as sin, it doesn't give you karma, and that is important. You are only punished by society and not by God.

4.4 Do not consume "wrongly"

And it is seen falsely as less sinful to show a massacre, like in some movies that top the movie charts, than a scene that is with a naked man or woman. The censor cuts out, what is too hot for him and that is some kind of dictatorship. They should cut out the cruelty shown so often and people would behave less cruel.

Further not only actions do give you karma, but thoughts and feelings too. You care about a healthy diet? You don't eat wrong food. You care about a healthy mind, then don't watch stupid movies or consume too much TV with scenes of cruelty and disaster. It is easy. Garbage in, garbage out. Stay clean.

Don't watch horror; don't watch movies of war and movies of crime. There should be a TV-channel with no-violent movies. You do not need to ignore "reality" but don't go into vicious circles no more.

There is crime and violence on TV, then people feel "inspired" and commit crime and violence, then again you have crime and violence on TV and so on. Get the war out of your heads!

5. A cleaning-ritual

For Jesus, as you see in the Papyrus Oxyrhynchus 840, the inner cleaning is the most important. He accepted the outer bath ritual, bud made clear that this is not enough.

What if you combine both? You can call me a heretic, but being a mystic, I do like the alchemy. If you combine the outer washing with internal cleaning, the internal cleaning is more easy and effectual.

Let's say you take a bath or shower before church, you can do so. Or my preferred idea is to integrate a cleaning ceremony into the life of church.

If there was a basin or an affluent fountain with several taps in a round, you would have the waters of the source (that is God) who symbolically clean the believer while he or she washes the hands in a ritual before the mass, thus cleansing him-/herself from sin and karma.

This could be made a ritual that is done regularly and not only once like baptism.

"Woman doing a cleaning-prayer in the river of Ganges"

6. The harvest: What it means to be clean

So what are the advantages of being clean?

Not to have dark spots on your garment is naturally seen as nice, but what is the advantage? Not to have binding karma frees you from the cycle of endless rebirth and you get a ticket for a seat at the house of god. You do not have to leave the house of God no more. You could, since will is free even with God, but you probably do not want to leave no more, since the house of God is shining beauty, endless abundance and all-fulfilling love.

To sum it up, you can clean up yourself from karma/sin, you can, and that is quite obvious, take a shower or bath before church or going to the temple which is like offering only the best to God and you better do both. To offer your best is a kind of "bakti" which means "love of god". When you are in love with someone, you bring her roses not the garbage.

With God it is paradoxically some kind of different too. You should give the best you are but as well as your worst sin and offer it to God too, so that God can help you to dispose of the darkest garbage of your soul. That is the ultimate karma cleansing.

If you meditate or contemplate or even reflect on yourself and you see what is not perfect or what you think is sin, take it into the prayer and ask God for forgiveness and ask God to help you to change for the better.

7. The Cross of Karma

"... Take up your cross, and follow me. ..." (Matthew 16:24), Jesus said. You first have to be true to yourself and accept that you have collected karma since you have sinned. You always have to recognize reality before you can change it.

"Jesus bearing his cross"

I say "you have collected karma" because the "concept of sin" as it is taught implies guilt. Guilt is a feeling that is like a glue. It sticks you to the cross.

The concept of karma is "sin-free". I prefer therefore the word "karma" since I want you to be free from the heavy burden of wrongdoing.

The heavy burden of your karma, "your sins", that is the cross that you bear.

The feeling of guilt is there to indicate that you have made a mistake. To make mistakes is human. So do not go into the feeling of guilt if you want to free yourself from sin. Try to understand what the lesson was you had to learn from that situation. If you understand the lesson, the karma can be cleaned.

The purpose of karma is to teach you something and not to punish you. Better think of God as a good teacher who shows you things you have not seen yet than in a punishing God.

God is mercy, not punishment.

And well, if you know "mercy", why don't you take Jesus from the cross? "As you sow so you shall reap". Remember, always when you free someone from their cross, you free yourself too. Do it in a way that does not hurt the other person.
Jesus cannot take your sins away, he can only help you to solve them yourself. Since it is your soul that

wants to learn the lesson. And it is your life.

When the mist of sins has gone and the veils of karma have cleared, the bride is ripe for communion with God. Then the source of all, the sun of sun again shines in the clear blue sky of your mind. Then you have overcome the cross of karma.

"The empty cross of Karma "

The role of Jesus is to show the way. You have to walk the way. Jesus cannot walk it for you. It is your life.

Sources:

Text:

Papyrus Oxyrhynchus 840: from "The other Gospels", Bart D. Ehrmann & Zlatako Plese, Oxford University Press 2014

Pictures:

page 2: "Washed from sin", Taufstein der Stadkirche Schorndorf/Germany, Frank Ludwig
page 4: "Fountain", Frankfurt/M, Frank Ludwig
page 5: "Pomegranate", Frank Ludwig
page 12: "Can you walk on water?", shutterstock
page 14: "Jesus washing sins", shutterstock
page 29 "Woman doing a cleaning-prayer in the river of Ganges": <a href="http://www.shutterstock.com/gallery-490933p1.html?cr=00&pl=edit-00">Pius Lee</a> / <a href="http://www.shutterstock.com/editorial?cr=00&pl=edit-00">Shutterstock.com</a>
page 31: "Jesus bearing his cross", shutterstock
page 33: "The empty cross of Karma ", shutterstock

The author

The author of this book, born 24.12.1966, studied Business Administration and Personal Coaching. He is a mystic and lives near Frankfurt/M, Germany. After studying Business Administration he turned to philosophy and later spirituality like Yoga, Hindu and Buddhist philosophy, Christian mystic and educated himself as Personal Coach. He works as a Personal coach and writes books.

The book

"The cross of karma: Comment on Papyrus Oxy V 840" comments Papyrus Oxyrhynchus 840 and describes in the following the possibilities and the impact of internal cleaning for ascending on the path to God.

Papyrus Oxyrhynchus 840 is a small piece of papyrus bearing 45 lines of text written shortly after the life of Jesus. It was found by Bernard Pyne Grennfell and Arthur Surridge Hunt in 1908 and is called an apocryptical gospel. You can find the original of the manuscript under Signature Ms. Gr. Th. G 11 in the Bodleian Library in Oxford/England.

The concept of karma is explained as synonym to that of sin, but without adding the poison of guilt, which serves as a glue to bind you to your sins, to bind you to your cross. Living a natural and humble life leads to sanity. Sanity leads to God.
If you accept that you are bound to sin, that means to err and to collect karma, you can clean yourself from that karma if you do not stick to guilt.

With guilt, you don't solve your karma, with the cross of your karma; you will not ascend to God.

Jesus cannot take your sins away; he can only help you to solve them yourself. Since it is your soul that wants to learn the lesson of life. And it is your life.